TIME TRAVELLERS
PIRATES

by Brian Williams
Consultant Richard Platt

ticktock
MEDIA

Copyright © ticktock Entertainment Ltd 2006
First published in Great Britain in 2005 by ticktock Media Ltd.,
Unit 2, Orchard Business Centre, North Farm Road, Tunbridge Wells, Kent TN2 3XF

ISBN 1 86007 610 6 pbk
Printed in China

A CIP catalogue record for this book is available from the British Library.

Picture credits (t=top; b=bottom; c=centre; l=left; r=right): Album Archivo Fotografico: 2-3, 4-5, 5tl, 8-9main, 9tl, 11l, 12tl, 14-15. Corbis: 7tr,
20-21. Heritage Image Partnership: 7tl (The British Library), 19br (The British Museum). National Maritime Museum: 10, 13br, 21tl, 22t, 23cr.
Royal Armouries: 15cr. Every effort has been made to trace the copyright holders and we apologise in advance for any unintentional omissions.
We would be pleased to insert the appropriate acknowledgement in any subsequent edition of this publication.

Contents

Glossary

On page 24 there is a glossary of words and terms. The glossary words appear in **bold** in the text.

Meet the pirates

Pirates were sea robbers who sailed the seas in search of treasure. There have been pirates at sea throughout history. When terrified sailors saw a ship flying a pirate flag, they knew they were about to be **ATTACKED!**

Some pirates were called **buccaneers**. Others were called **corsairs** or **privateers**.

A buccaneer pirate

The actor Johnny Depp in the film Pirates of the Caribbean.

Privateers were pirates who actually worked for their **government**. They attacked the ships of enemy countries.

4

About three hundred years ago there were lots of pirates at sea. There were even women pirates who dressed as men.

Life on-board a **navy ship** or **merchant ship** was sometimes so tough that ordinary sailors chose to become pirates instead!

Some pirates were runaway **slaves**. Others were crooks who took to the sea to escape the law.

Pirate facts

Pirate ships flew flags with pictures that stood for death! The flags were called JOLLY ROGERS.

In ancient times, the Roman navy CHASED PIRATES around the Mediterranean Sea.

THE VIKINGS were pirates who sailed the seas in their longships.

Famous pirates

A life spent stealing treasure might sound exciting, but many famous pirates came to **A STICKY END!**

Blackbeard (real name Edward Teach) was a pirate who attacked ships in the Caribbean. Blackbeard's evil ways terrified sailors and his own **crew!**

Blackbeard the pirate in battle.

When Blackbeard was cornered by the British navy in 1718, it took five gunshots and 20 **cutlass** cuts to kill him!

Welshman Bartholomew Roberts (known as Black Bart) was one of the most successful pirates ever. He captured over 400 ships in his career.

Captain Bartholomew Roberts

Captain William Kidd worked for the English **government**, hunting for pirates. However, Kidd's crew of cut-throats made him turn into a pirate. In the end, the English government hanged Kidd for piracy!

Captain William Kidd

Women pirates

Englishwoman MARY READ became a pirate disguised as a man!

So did ANNE BONNY. The two women sailed on pirate Jack Rackham's ship in the Caribbean.

When captured, both women escaped hanging because they were pregnant!

Come aboard

Pirates went to sea in wooden sailing ships. They liked small, fast ships which could catch large, slow **galleons**. Pirates also needed fast ships to make QUICK GETAWAYS.

At sea, the pirate **crew** had to work hard, tugging on ropes to fix the ship's sails. The sails trapped wind that drove the ship along. A pirate ship's top speed was about 17 miles an hour.

Many pirate ships leaked because underwater worms ate holes in the wooden bottoms of the ships.

The actor Johnny Depp with a ship's wheel!

Pirate ships were steered by a wheel that moved a big underwater **rudder**.

Captain Kidd's ship was called the *Adventure Galley*. It had room on-board for 150 men. The ship was 38 metres long and had 34 **cannon**.

A reconstruction of a pirate ship. Note the Jolly Roger flag!

Sailing ship artefacts

The captain used a COMPASS to show him which direction the ship was sailing in.

The ship's ANCHOR hooked into the seabed to keep the ship in one place.

Life on a pirate ship

Life at sea was **DANGEROUS**. Some ships sank in storms and everyone drowned. Sometimes pirates killed one another in quarrels over treasure. Men fell overboard, caught diseases or starved when the food or fresh water ran out.

Sometimes, pirates got so hungry they cooked and ate their leather belts and shoes!

A ship's biscuit, also called hardtack.

The ship's cook made **salt-meat** stews over a wood fire in the **galley**. The stew was eaten with hard biscuits that often had maggots wriggling inside!

Life at sea was also very smelly! Nobody washed and the drinking water went bad. The toilet was a hole in the ship's deck, overhanging the sea.

Only the captain had his own **cabin**. The **crew** slept in **hammocks** which they rolled up during the day.

A pirate captain with two crewmen from a pirate film.

Pirate food and drink

Food and drinking water were stored in wooden **BARRELS**.

Pirates took **CHICKENS** to sea with them for eggs.

The **SHIP'S GOAT** produced milk.

Choose your weapon

To look fierce, pirates carried **LOTS OF WEAPONS.**
When they went into battle, they fired guns, threw
grenades and slashed at people with **cutlasses** and
daggers. Many ships' **crews** surrendered rather
than fight back!

Ships firing cannon, from the film
Pirates of the Caribbean.

Pirate ships had
big guns called
cannon. The
cannon fired
cannon balls
made of iron.

This flintlock pistol took about 30 seconds to load.

A pirate's flintlock **pistol**
only fired one shot, then it
needed reloading. So in a battle,
each pirate carried five or six pistols!

Pirates used axes to chop through ropes and smash through **cabin** doors when they were searching for treasure.

A Corsair pirate with an axe, cutlass and pistols.

Cannon made a lot of **NOISE AND SMOKE**, but they were hard to aim.

When they hit a ship, **CANNON BALLS** made showers of splinters which could kill people.

A **PIRATE'S CUTLASS** was short, so it was easy to swing on a crowded deck.

Attack!

Sneaky pirates often played tricks on other ships. At sea, they pretended to be peaceful **cargo** ships until they were close to another ship. Then... up went THE JOLLY ROGER!

Cannons boomed as the pirates opened fire, trying to hit the other ship to stop it escaping.

When they got close, the pirates threw ropes with grappling irons across to the other ship to pull the two ships together. Then they rushed into battle!

A pirate attack from the movie Pirates of the Caribbean.

Sometimes pirates would sneak into a **port** and take over a ship while its **crew** were asleep.

Pirate artefacts

GRAPPLING IRONS, attached to ropes, hooked in the rigging (ropes) of the ship under attack.

Chain shot, fired by cannon, SMASHED the other ship's masts and sails.

The pirate BLACKBEARD tied lighted gunpowder fuses in his hair to look extra scary in battle.

Pirate treasure

When they ATTACKED A SHIP, pirates hoped to find gold, silver and jewels. But they also stole silks, pearls, fine clothes, fresh food, weapons and the ship's medicine chest!

After an attack, the pirates shared out the treasure. The captain always got the biggest share!

Pirates would steal a ship's ropes and sails to replace their own. Sometimes pirates would even keep a ship if it was better than their own.

Only pirates in stories buried their treasure on desert islands. Real pirates spent all their loot on having a good time!

Pirate artefacts

Silver coins called **PIECES OF EIGHT** could be cut into pieces to be shared out.

A ship's medicine chest contained medicines for treating diseases and **BATTLE WOUNDS.**

A **GOLD DOUBLOON** (coin) was worth about seven weeks **wages** to an ordinary sailor.

Pirate kingdoms

Pirates met up in **HIDEOUTS** where they could rest and have some fun. They also had to clean and repair their ships. If a huge band of pirates lived together, no **navy** ship dared attack them!

The Caribbean and the Mediterranean were busy pirate hideouts!

North America

Europe

Mediterranean Sea

Atlantic Ocean

Caribbean Sea

Africa

South America

Port Royal in Jamaica was a famous pirate den. A **buccaneer** pirate called Henry Morgan led an army of pirates from here.

On shore, pirates liked getting drunk and **gambling** with cards and dice.

Pirates needed to clean **barnacles** and seaweed from the hulls (bottoms) of their ships. This was called *careening*. To do this, the pirates pulled the ship onto its side in shallow water.

Pirate artefacts

KEEP AWAY!
The Jolly Rogers on this map show the places where pirate hideouts could be found.

Asia

South China Sea

Pacific Ocean

Indian Ocean

Australia

This bottle is three hundred years old. It contained wine or rum – popular PIRATE DRINKS!

These playing cards came from a pirate ship. GAMBLING was a quick way to lose all your treasure!

Pirate punishments

The punishment for piracy was **DEATH BY HANGING**. Pirates were hanged on a **gallows**. A captured pirate could sometimes win a **pardon** by "telling" on his **crew** mates.

PIRATE SHIP RULES:

No fighting with other crew members.

No candles or smoking near the **cargo**.

No stealing from crew mates.

Pirates had their own rules. A pirate who broke the ship's rules might be marooned – left behind on a desert island to starve to death.

This painting shows a prisoner in leg irons.

Pirates put leg irons on their prisoners to stop them running away. If prisoners were rich, they could sometimes be ransomed (exchanged for money).

Pirates were cruel to the **officers** of the ships they captured – especially if they thought the officers had been cruel to their crew.

Some pirates carried out terrible punishments such as cutting off their prisoners' lips and ears.

Pirate artefacts

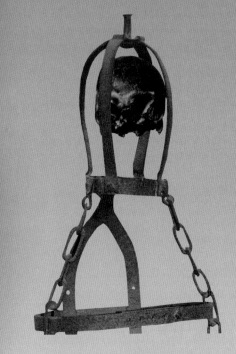

A hanged pirate's **DEAD BODY** was hung up in an iron cage as a warning to others.

A pirate who disobeyed his captain was **FLOGGED** with a whip called a cat o' nine tails.

21

A world of pirates

The **Caribbean Sea** was a favourite haunt for pirates, but ships could be attacked anywhere in the world. **Cargo** ships sailed along regular routes, so pirates **LURKED** where they knew ships would pass.

The **Barbary Corsairs** of the Mediterranean didn't just steal treasure. They also kidnapped men they could sell and use as **slaves**.

Corsairs went to sea in **galleys** rowed by slaves.

Corsair pirates in battle.

Pirates of the Caribbean attacked Spanish treasure ships packed with gold from Mexico and Peru.

A golden mask from Peru.

Chinese pirates in **junks** chased cargo ships across the Indian Ocean and South China Sea.

A Chinese pirate king called Ching-Chi-ling led a fleet of 1,000 junks.

A model of a Chinese junk.

Pirate facts

When food ran out on Chinese pirate ships, the pirates and their prisoners had to EAT RATS with their rice!

In battle, galleys would RAM (smash into) the sides of other ships.

Asian pirates fought with dao swords decorated with a lock of hair from A DEAD ENEMY.

23

Glossary

ARTEFACTS Items made by people. For example an anchor or weapon.

BARBARY CORSAIRS Pirates from the Berber or 'Barbary' coast of North Africa.

BARNACLES Small sea creatures with hard shells, that cling to rocks or boats.

BUCCANEERS Pirates of the Caribbean. The name came from a kind of barbecue the pirates used, called a *boucan*.

CABIN A small room on a ship for living and sleeping in.

CANNON Big guns loaded with gunpowder. They fired cannon balls (iron balls).

CARGO Goods carried on a ship.

CORSAIRS French and Mediterranean pirates.

CREW Sailors who work on a ship.

CUTLASS A short sword.

GALLEONS Sailing ships with three masts.

GALLEY A ship's kitchen. Also the name for a ship with sails and oars.

GALLOWS Wooden frame for executions by hanging.

GAMBLING Playing cards and dice games for money.

GOVERNMENT The people who run a country.

GRENADES Small, gunpowder-filled bombs.

HAMMOCKS Beds made from cloth and rope, hung from hooks.

JUNKS Chinese sailing ships with sails that look like window blinds.

MERCHANT SHIP A ship loaded with cargo.

NAVY SHIP A warship belonging to a country.

OFFICERS People who give orders on a ship.

PARDON Being forgiven or "let off" for doing something wrong.

PISTOL A small hand gun that fires balls of lead.

PORT A place where ships load and unload cargo.

PRIVATEERS Pirates who worked for a government against an enemy country.

RUDDER A large, wide, flat part which could be tilted from side to side to steer a ship.

SALT-MEAT Meat kept in salty water to make it last longer.

SLAVES People who were owned by other people. Slaves had to work for their masters.

WAGES Money paid to someone in return for work.

Index